A Taste of Glory:

Explorations Into
John 6:53-58

Donald Charles Lacy

Fairway Press, Lima, Ohio

A TASTE OF GLORY

FIRST EDITION
Copyright © 2000 by
Donald Charles Lacy

Library of Congress Catalog Card Number: 99-96991

ISBN 0-7880-1495-1
          PRINTED IN U.S.A.

Dedication

Anne Marie Lacy,
confirmed in Saint Athanasius Catholic Church
in Evanston, Illinois,
and resting in the love of God
in Catholic Calvary Cemetery
on the shores of Lake Michigan

Table Of Contents

Prelude   7

The Truth (John 6:53)   11

Eternal Life (John 6:54)   17

Food And Drink (John 6:55)   25

Real Presence (John 6:56)   31

Living Father (John 6:57)   37

From Heaven (John 6:58)   45

Postlude   53

Prelude

Pilgrim: Precious and loving Lord, I need a special visit with You again. For some time now I have been pondering the glorious words that come from Saint John's Gospel in the sixth chapter. I mean, of course, verses 53 through 58.

Jesus: You know I love you and will listen carefully.

Pilgrim: Dear Jesus, that's why I came to You again. Every time I read these words I am taken up into a magnificent world of powerful mystery. I just have a really tough time explaining how I feel. Your flesh and Your blood! O great and holy One, I kneel in humble adoration. Please help me to understand, at least, in an elementary fashion what this is all about.

Jesus: Remember, my son, it takes genuine humility and sincerity to begin to know Me better.

Pilgrim: So many times over the years I have experienced Your body and blood in Holy Communion as a dull act of scheduled worship, yearning to be free. There was so much more to be felt and appreciated! It is as though You desired deeply to be so much closer and meaningful but just couldn't. This makes me so sad. There was an awesome greatness and powerful love waiting to burst forth but, Lord, it just didn't happen! In agony I watched and waited. Decent people went through the motions. Some, including myself, even knelt in prayer but it just didn't happen.

Jesus: I gave and continue to give My body. I gave and continue to give My blood. Do you and others actually want to eat My flesh and drink My blood from My priests and pastors or deep down do you only seek a bit of solace for the moment?

7

Pilgrim: Please be merciful to me, Lord. I want all the spiritual grandeur these verses from Saint John's Gospel offer. I long for that perfect promised closeness. Sometimes in great pain I suffer to have this unique gift of Yourself that guarantees Your true presence. Lord, I beg of You, please hear me out. The Holy Spirit is moving mightily in my life and others. We believe our desire comes from undefiled motivation. I am not afraid, only frustrated and disappointed by the Holy Communion being so much less than what I believe You surely intended. Your children seem to be often sitting at a banquet table offering Your flesh and blood but they are starving, or at least, seriously malnourished!

Jesus: Do you remember what I said to you recently? Let me refresh your memory: "Do not judge others and God will not judge you. Do not condemn others and God will not condemn you. Forgive others and God will forgive you." Think on this and focus on My Crucifixion.

Pilgrim: Savior of my soul, please forgive again all my sins of omission and commission. I trust You with my life and death. I want somehow for Your body to become my body. I want some way for Your blood to become my blood. I give You myself — fully, totally, and completely. I really have nothing else to offer.

Jesus: Are you sure there are no reservations? So just what will you try to hide in hopes I will not notice? Will an old love and preoccupation entice you to treat My body and My blood as merely a means to the ends of self glory? Reflect upon My conversation with Simon Peter near the end of John's Gospel.

Pilgrim: Lord, be merciful to me, a sinner who wavers under pressure! I do not deserve what I ask. Even my spiritual riches are pitiful rags in Your sight. Even my most lofty motivations and ideals leave something to be desired. Even my humility and sincerity sometimes turn to pride. Even my thought patterns and ways of behaving reveal a life struggling just enough to be decent in the world's sight. I plead with You, be merciful and do for me what I can never do for myself. Yes, Lord, I truly want more than anything else Your body and Your blood. Lord, do what You will.

Jesus: Very well, my son. You have learned much. Today your spiritual journey becomes one of joyful obedience and sacrificial love. My Body and My blood shall sustain you. Do not look back. My love will never let you go.

I

THE TRUTH

Jesus said to them, *"I tell you the truth, unless you eat the flesh of the Son of Man and drink his blood, you have no life in you."*　　　John 6:53 (NIV)

INTRODUCTION

How strange these words seem to many who profess the Name of Christ!

I can remember a number of years ago how this caught my attention and fascination. It was something I didn't understand and yet could not turn loose. It not only intrigued me but sometimes even haunted me. I would ask myself, "The truth of what?" My own background was such that it seemed these words were simply a spiritualizing by Saint John of our pilgrimage with Christ. To connect them to a Sacrament we utilized once every quarter in a very symbolic way was a misinterpretation of Holy Scripture. How can anyone seriously connect *the truth* with eating flesh and drinking blood, even if it is Christ's. This must be a suggestive and meditative way for us to pray, go to church, and give generously of our money! But that seemed superficial and a denial of miracle that the Bible certainly talked about. Perhaps a subtle but ever-present anti-Catholic assumption had entered my thought processes back there someplace!

FOCUS

If Jesus is telling us *the truth*, just what is it? What do we make of such seemingly strange words, yes, and even foreign to the way we may understand our precious Faith? I share with you probing that I have felt necessary and provided spiritual growth.

APPLICATION

Pay close attention to what is being said

If you are attempting to read this verse like the latest edition of *USA Today*, forget it! If you are relaxing with a Jane Austen novel and decide to read this verse briefly for your devotional time, forget it! If you are watching Dan Rather's news commentary and try to ponder this verse during commercials, forget it! If you reflect upon it between innings of a Cubs' game, forget it! If you carry it with you all day long and plead with Jesus for help, praise God!

To be focused on *the truth* is so necessary. Today's living tends to divide us into compartments, which has given rise to some strange and even immoral ways of behavior. I believe with all of my heart that Jesus taught holiness and that means wholeness in ways that enable us to be healthy and productive people. This, of course, does not mean we try to explain to our employers or supervisors we are paying so much attention to John 6:53 we just can't do our work for which we are paid. It does mean it has found a place in our hearts, minds, and souls where our subconscious life values it very highly, always seeking more light on the matter.

So, Jesus says He is telling us *the truth*. That means *pay close attention to what is being said.*

Be humble and teachable

If we are going to mine riches of Holy Scripture, I am not sure there are any more significant words than "humble" and "teachable." I have often insisted we must come to Holy Scripture either figuratively or literally on our knees. Anything less almost certainly is guaranteed not to help us. The verse we are exploring is an excellent example. Actually, the best prayer of which I am aware is simply to say, "Lord, what is it you want me to know with the guidance of your Holy Spirit? Please come to me. I am ready to learn. I will value every moment. Please come to me." The necessity of brilliant theology in many languages has always fascinated

12

me. But if we are only fascinated by brilliant theology, is that not eventually futile?

I beg of you not to consider *the truth* as solely a one-on-one relationship with God that ignores enlightened and powerful teachers. To be sure Jesus is the Master teacher through the Holy Spirit but beware of a private interpretation that another Christian has neither seen nor in any way been given opportunity to give his/her witness to it. Even humility and teachability can be redirected to manifest pride and self-righteousness.

So Jesus says He is telling us *the truth*. That means be *humble and teachable*.

Avoid "inherited" agenda that suffocates.

Is there anyone who thinks he/she has an open mind free from "inherited" agenda? This inquiry is not necessarily negative because how else are we given moral, ethical, and spiritual principles to live by? The point is as we move through life and hope, as Saint Paul says, to become a "mature man in Christ" that we test those areas of our thinking that are barriers and even barricades. To hold too tightly to some theological interpretation that freezes out a bigger picture and closer walk with Christ is sometimes even more than spiritual suffocation; it is demonic. Introspection of one's thinking, in my experience, is almost always profitable. *The truth* of which our Lord is speaking means we must be willing to give up cherished belief under the guidance of the Holy Spirit.

The magnificence and mystery of the Holy Communion is always more than any of our "inherited" agendas. God honors our search for *the truth*. To test our ways and beliefs is a kind of blessed questing that should aid our growth dynamic. So often as Christians we seem to be bogged down and thwarted by refusing to let go of long-standing viewpoints that really only perpetuate half-truths and less. A healthy ecumenism is very helpful!

So, Jesus says He is telling us *the truth*. That means *avoid "inherited" agenda that suffocates*.

Give yourself totally to the sacrifice of Christ.

"Sacrifice" is a word built into the very fabric of the Judeo-Christian revelation. In our case being disciples of the Christ the word takes on a meaning powerful and loving — pointing directly to the Holy Communion and the Crucifixion. We learn that God's Son literally gives His body and blood for us. This is a sacrifice clearly above any other event in history because it provides for our right relationship with the Father through the Son. The gift of the innocent Lamb of God for you and me draws us to a single happening, doing something for us we could never do for ourselves. We are called by a love beyond human comprehension to give ourselves to the Crucified One. A crucifix held closely to our bodies with gratitude and concentration begins to get at this marvelous gift!

I believe those who are fully committed to Christ and His Church are immersed spiritually in Christ's sacrifice. Saint Paul helps us by proclaiming he "decided to know nothing but Jesus Christ and Him crucified." Among other things we enter into pain and joy that mixes to become a means for us to be more than bystanders of the Faith. We can know in our depths *the truth* of His body and blood for our pilgrimage is never a matter of option. It is imperative and always at the very core of our redemption.

So, Jesus says He is telling us *the truth*. That means *give yourself totally to the sacrifice of Christ.*

Forgive those who have misled you.

If you have had similar experiences to mine in the life of the churches, you have been afflicted by a mindset that seriously devaluated the Lord's Supper. *The truth* is for generations many have refused *the truth* of our Blessed Lord as recorded in John 6:53. Among numerous groups who call themselves "Protestants," "independents," "fundamentalists," "evangelicals," etc., the Sacrament has frequently been depicted a corrupt relic coming out of liturgically-oriented bodies of Christians. Indeed, some would not

14

even call them Christians! Anything more than bread, grape juice, and symbolism was suspect. Be forgiving and give thanks for the progress being made under the guidance of Holy Spirit.

History bears witness to the evil of men and women "using" the Holy Scriptures for their own means and ends. Those who have considered Roman Catholics and Orthodox less than Christian, even pagan, seem almost invariably bent on committing the same infractions they accuse these two groups of doing! Who has not heard a "preacher" issue his/her own encyclical? Who has not observed a "called and inspired minister" cling tenaciously to his/her own dogma? Who has not witnessed those, clergy and laity, maintain they are their own popes? As we trust in the guidance of the Holy Spirit, we are called to forgive those who have knowingly or unknowingly misled us. Yet, let us not be unaware of our own temptation to pontificate! So much is at stake, indeed, our very souls.

So, Jesus says He is telling us *the truth*. That means *forgive those who have misled you.*

CONCLUSION

Isn't this just an incredible verse! It teases and tantalizes our spirituality. It invigorates our walk with the Lord. It causes us to cry out in painful joy, "I want *the truth*, Lord." It moves us into an arena of understanding that disregards our comfort zones. It promises us more than we have ever dreamed. It has a blessedness about it that thrills with tears of thanksgiving. Sometimes I perceive our Lord is saying, "Come to Me, all you who are weak and heavy laden with a mere taste of glory, and I will give you more, much more." *The truth*, Lord; yes, we want (beg for) *the truth*, Lord.

EXPLORATION

1. How can I improve my concentration on the Lord's Word?

2. Are my humility and being willing to be taught genuine?

3. Am I willing to take a serious and ongoing look at my assumptions?

4. Why is the sacrifice of my Lord so important?

5. What does the Lord mean by "forgiving others and God will forgive you"?

II

ETERNAL LIFE

*"Whoever eats my flesh and drinks my blood has
eternal life, and I will raise him up at the last day."*
John 6:54 (NIV)

INTRODUCTION

Generally speaking, *eternal life* simply means life beyond this life.

In our precious Faith it means Resurrection and unending time with our Savior and Lord. While the very early followers of Christ seemed to expect His virtually immediate return to this earth, they did not disown the Faith in large numbers because it didn't happen. Certainly in the inspired Word that comes from Saint John we note a direct link to Holy Communion. To receive His body and blood is to be a part of life beyond the grave. This suggests a spiritual power that is a necessity for peace and happiness in the hereafter. I suppose there are millions of professing Christians who find real difficulty with that. Not only would they deny its necessity they would not even consider the Sacrament imperative for living the Christian life! In my understanding this is a huge and even crucial problem that needs to be solved as we grope towards Christian Unity. You and I might like to have it some other way but — like so many facets of truth coming to the surface in our day — we are confronted by ancient Catholic understanding. The Holy Spirit is much at work!

FOCUS

What can we do to move beyond the text and begin to get ahold of some ideas that are beneficial for us? Maybe we will create more problems than we can solve! Yet, it is through testing and questing we get a firm grip on Biblical interpretation. Perhaps the asking of relevant questions is the most helpful.

APPLICATION

Is our Lord referring to something other than the Sacrament of Holy Communion?

If He is, then what is it? Perhaps we can stretch ourselves into believing we are dealing with a purely spiritual matter that does not involve in any way liturgy and elements. Therefore, this whole business of *eternal life* can be seen as related solely to various disciplines such as prayer, congregational worship, and tithing. Of course, we would not want to leave out the gift of the "new birth" which some say the Sacrament has no connection whatsoever to our prior condition or conditions after "being saved." In other words, salvation comes to us and stays with us with the assurance of *eternal life* with or without the Holy Communion. Some seem to have a certain distaste for anything other than one-on-one with God who relays to them a spiritual perception that needs no corporate approval!

Obviously, if we can move the Sacrament away from the essentials of our spiritual livelihood, we can divorce it from heavenly bliss. It seems to me we can also open the door to a privatized understanding that becomes exceedingly self-centered. For some I have known this avenue takes them away from awful images of priests, chalices, and structured liturgy! While one's individualism is a priceless commodity, is it a reason to deny common agreement that has been with God's people since the time of Christ and His Apostles? It's almost like maintaining "I have found the way to *eternal life*, so please don't bother me about what others have found true."

So, *is our Lord referring to something other than the Sacrament of Holy Communion*? My prayer life and studies answer strongly in the negative.

18

Why is it necessary to lock together the here and now with the hereafter?

Isn't the Eucharist a taste of the glory to come? Over the centuries followers of the Christ have discovered this to be true by their own experience. Perhaps this is why many of us have such difficulty. We have never experienced the mysterious magnificence of being at one with the "cloud of witnesses" who have gone before us. Perhaps the Lord's Supper is just an important act of worship set in a moment of time on this earth with no relationship to the Church Triumphant. Life and death are separated in ways that transcending these meager moments on this earth are seen as impossible.

Does Holy Communion have anything to do with the "resurrection of the body and the life everlasting"? Certainly the words coming from Saint John believes it does. Do you and I? From a pastoral point of view — I have discovered in my churches, all Methodist or United Methodist — an ongoing fragmenting of both worship and doctrine. In short, far too often I have heard, "I came to hear the sermon and am not really interested in what comes before or after." There is a tendency to reduce worship to a speech-making that provides help for coping with life. There is little or no thought given to solid, ancient doctrine. Our churches need pastors who are also resident theologians who will stay more than two years at each appointment! Of course, it takes a pastoral heart to do serious and significant teaching, plus lay co-operation.

So, *why is it necessary to lock together the here and now with the hereafter*? Precisely because that is the Word from the Lord.

Aren't there some alternatives to John's rendering of what Jesus said?

Pastor, "You are just too literal." Maybe that happens to be your viewpoint. Maybe you would prefer this passage to be put in a devotional context that avoids altogether the dealing with the Sacrament. Visions of *eternal life* are summoned and you say to yourself, "What does that have to do with bread and grape juice?" I will grant you that interpretation and application of scriptural passages can be extremely difficult. However, I can also witness to the fact many, many professing His name have been plagued with prejudices that have taken away the power the ancient Church found in this passage. Our oldest known reference to Holy Communion is found in the 11th Chapter of Saint Paul's First Letter to the Corinthians. It speaks, among other things, of not recognizing the meaning found in the Sacrament, thereby eating and drinking judgment on himself.

Why don't we just enjoy the verse in our Bible reading and devotions, avoiding unnecessary controversy? This way we can just leave it as a lofty statement that remains an enigma to us. Well, that sounds pretty good, doesn't it? The problem with that is the weight of Christian history, theology, and practice is solidly against us! The strong connection between the Eucharist, Mass, or Holy Communion and *eternal life* has been with us since the earliest of times in the life of the church. To move the altar from a prominent and central place, replacing it with the pulpit, may be an attempt to correct abuses. But since when did moving church furniture around change deeply imbedded doctrine? I believe preaching to be sacramental under the guidance of the Holy Spirit. I do not believe it acts as a substitute for what Saint John conveys.

So, *aren't there some alternatives to John's rendering of what Jesus said*? Well, perhaps, but their validity is questionable.

Does avoiding and evading the Sacrament seriously decrease one's chance of going to heaven?

What sort of a question is that! "Are you implying I might go to hell just because I don't think Communion is important?" might very well be your response. Well, it appears to me the question has to be posed because of the emphasis placed on it by Holy Scripture. For example, we read in all three of the synoptic Gospels the story of the institution of this Sacrament. An early letter (1st Corinthians) of Saint Paul also tells us of the institution. How can

20

we possibly say it is not important? In terms of revelation as doctrine and a way of living our lives, don't we look at the Gospels first and foremost? Then we consult the remainder of the *New Testament*. I believe that is the general understanding or mind of the Universal Church. "Do this in remembrance of Me" must not be taken lightly. Can we even say, "Lord, I want to go to heaven but don't tell me to take Your Supper as an imperative for getting there."

In the contemporary mindset of various churches are we posing a question that is considered irrelevant? I have a strong feeling that is truly the case. *Eternal life* is not really among the top considerations in the lives of numerous persons confessing the Christian Faith. At least, this is my observations and experience. To connect the Sacrament with *eternal life* may only add to the irrelevance! So much of popular worship is built along the lines of not only "feel good" theology but expressions and organizations barely based in revelation.

So, *does avoiding and evading the Sacrament seriously decrease one's chance of going to heaven?* To be sure, only God is our Judge but we are called to be faithful, especially to the Gospels and the *New Testament*.

What does this issue and topic have to say about the teaching of various denominations?

Talk about opening Pandora's box! I suppose there is no single individual who can come close to giving us a full accounting and description that would encompass all views, including some elementary understanding of practices. I dare say the concept of Holy Communion would be found in all who profess the Christ. Its power and relevance would run the gamut. Its relationship to *eternal life* might even run a wider gamut! With the numerous independent ministries today we find worship activities that stagger the imagination. Yet, it is my responsibility to be faithful to the ancient revelation and all that entails.

My spiritual travels and personal pilgrimage, including professional integrity, tell me we must stay close to the teachings of not only our Lord and the Apostles but to the ancient Catholic wellsprings of the earliest centuries. In a more complete sense the Orthodox wellsprings have to be included as well. To partake of this eucharistic banquet as a serious disciple of the Christ is to sample in a limited way the heavenly celebration. I believe this is to be, at least, some of the bedrock we have been consistently provided by both our Catholic and Orthodox friends.

So, *what does this issue and topic have to say about the teaching of various denominations*? One is not as good as another and we are driven to Christ, the Apostolic witness, and the Church Fathers (East and West) for answers that stand the test of times.

CONCLUSION

As we close this visit, are we prodded to "come clean" in our attitudes and practices? The Word from the Lord through Saint John is that *eternal life* and His life-giving Sacrament are intended to be inseparable. I receive that as a great joy that lifts us above communion services that are afflicted by "funeral dirge" actions and reactions or light heartedness that strip the Sacrament of its power. Note how privileged and blessed we are as we are open to the Holy Spirit! Our Lord does not want us malnourished and impoverished but healthy and truly blessed by all that is intended for us.

EXPLORATION

1. Am I sometimes guilty of trying to explain away what the Lord intends?

2. Why are His Body and Blood a heavenly event?

3. What dangers do you see in the departure from ancient understanding and practice?

4. How is it possible to separate Holy Communion from eternal life?

5. Have you really explored your denomination's understanding of the Sacrament?

III

FOOD AND DRINK

*"For my flesh is real food and my blood is real
drink."*   John 6:55 (NIV)

INTRODUCTION

Our lives are made up of food and drink because that's just the
way things are!

Our Lord speaks to us in ways that begin with common de-
nominators. Will you and I be eating today? Unless we are fasting
or very ill, the answer will be a nonchalant, "Well, of course." Will
we be drinking today? This time the answer will be an even bigger, "Well, of course." I am not sure how long we can live without
liquids but it must be very brief. Jesus the Christ does not take any
chances with experiences that could be foreign to His sons and
daughters. In stark simplicity He could have prefaced these words
of the text by saying, "All of you eat and drink, so please listen to
the point I am going to make." This is so like our Savior, isn't it?
He seeks to relate to us on a level common and necessary for all. It
seems to me sometimes we work at misunderstanding Him! It also
seems to me there are many times Satan so clouds basic and fundamental revelation that we are left in a dither about things that destroy or seriously cripple our spiritual living. Praises be to the
Father for giving us His Son to speak in ways familiar and routine!

FOCUS

I want to know much more about this glorious simplicity, don't
you? I suggest to you we must attempt this in a plain and simple
commentary of our own. Positive and helpful statements about

25

our Lord's Supper will be our *modus operandi.* This may be more challenging than you and I suspect!

APPLICATION

Bread and wine were as natural as breathing the air.

Throughout the Hebrew Scriptures and the *New Testament* we discover people partaking of both at all levels of society. Bread was seen as the minimum to human subsistence. A common experience was the daily baking of bread. It was said Palestinian loaves looked like stones in the desert. Thus, we can make sense of our Lord's temptation to turn stones into bread. It was both leavened and unleavened. That which was unleavened was a reminder to the Hebrews of the haste of their Exodus from Egypt. Bread was an omnipresent commodity and recognized by all as necessary to life. Recall, even our Lord refers to Himself as "the bread of life" in a passage just prior to the verses we are studying for this series. What could have been more basic to life commonly understood than bread? Probably nothing.

Apparently there was a large variety of wine that found its way across all classes of people. In Genesis we note Melchizedek brought wine — along with bread — to Abraham. Of course, honesty requires we note the overindulgence of it produced numerous problems, some very serious. Yet, the *New Testament* tells us Jesus drank it and certainly must have used it to institute His Supper. The wedding at Cana gives us a glimpse of normal patterns at festivities and shows our Lord as something of a true social being who must have found enjoyment in such an environment. When we look at numbers among Christian worshipers, there are far more receiving wine in place of grape juice. This is largely because of frequency among Roman Catholics, Orthodox, Lutherans, and Anglicans. It is also true because they far outnumber other professing Christians.

So, *bread and wine were as natural as breathing air.* How fitting for "the Sacrament among Sacraments!

A person's flesh and blood indicated one's humanity.

In a very fundamental way how can one be any closer to a person than to speak on his body and blood? Like it or not, that is who we are and how we are constituted on this planet. Facial expressions are often what we remember about people. The grimace, the smile, the frown, the wonderment, and many others are preserved in our memories. The movement of his/her body still cause reactions long after the death angel had claimed the person. We know blood to be absolutely necessary for life. The ancient Hebrews and those around Jesus in His time not only knew blood to be imperative but related to it as both mysterious and mystical. Today's Christians would do well to imitate them! Think how precious and holy Jesus the Christ was to them. Try to imagine this precious and holy figure on the Cross dying for the sins of humanity. His Body was crucified and His Blood was shed.

One of the most majestically beautiful and awesomely powerful effects of His death was his human personhood. He was a genuine human being with His Body dying and His Blood running freely. They could relate to that! In our so-called "sanitized" environment can you and I relate to that? It is said our own ancestors fifty years ago and longer were much closer to death than we are because no one went to a hospital, unless death was almost a certainty. Nursing homes and even retirement facilities were quite scarce. Even with the truly great ministries done by both, perhaps we would benefit from the flesh and blood contact our ancestors knew first hand.

So, *a person's flesh and blood indicated one's humanity*. How distinctively precious was our Lord's Sacrifice!

"Real" food and "real" drink speak of unquestionable validity.

I believe the text seeks to make not only a memorable point but provide an everlasting sum and substance for all who would call Him Savior and Lord. Words alone fail to communicate the exalting gift presented to them nearly two thousand years ago, to us as of this moment, and all in between. Anything nominal and superficial seems so terribly out of place. Some of us can relate to such irreverence and perhaps blasphemous times in a service of worship that provided "communion"! Recall the experimentations of those attempting to be contemporary and up-to-date.

This is a time of kneeling before a truth at once both powerfully appealing and mightily alienating. The Faith community is called to the former. Those who find the whole idea repugnant find their place in the latter. Those may not be as far as apart as we first think! My heart, mind, and soul find it powerfully appealing. In fact, this is so true I tend to be lifted into another more captivating environment. How about you? I hope and pray you are not afflicted with repugnance. I am trusting in God that you not succumb to alienation.

So, *"real" food and "real" drink speak of unquestionable validity.* How truly secure we ought to feel!

"My" flesh and "My" blood move us into a very special relationship.

Can anything or anyone be more deeply personal than this? Our Savior and Lord wanted the Apostles and Christian Community to know: This is "My" flesh and this is "My" blood. He wants you and me to know precisely the same thing. The message is essentially unchanged. Our lives are brief. They are not much more than the blinking of an eye on the grand scale of time. We are privileged to have a constant. His flesh and blood are with us as people are born and die. Natural cycles continue their often predictable ways. Human beings rise and fall. "The" Sacrament remains with all of us, beckoning us into that relationship that calls for primacy.

I must confess to you there is much I do not understand here! At the same moment I freely admit there is also a great deal I do understand and appreciate beyond words that can be conveyed.

The intimacy is thrilling. The boldness of spiritual truth is breathtaking. The irrational, reckless way our Lord comes to us is brazen beyond compare. No wonder the pagan world labeled those Christians a bunch of cannibals! Those people eat some god's flesh and drink the blood! Do we catch a glimpse of how wonderfully blessed we are? And to think for some, they will pass into eternity never having recognized this!

So, *"My" flesh and "My" blood move us into a special relationship.* How can we want or need anything more profound!

We are in touch with ancient and essential revelation.

Saint John's Gospel, especially these few verses from the sixth chapter, has a way of singularly speaking to us. We read the synoptic Gospels and then John. Wow! We read the words of the institution of the Lord's Supper in the synoptic Gospels and Saint Paul's First Letter to the Corinthians. Then we read these few verses from John under consideration, especially verse 55. Wow! We stand on holy ground and in this verse the sublime uniqueness of it is a marvel to behold. God is so good for us! We are allowed into profundity the ancient Hebrews never knew but perhaps partially expected. So, much has been given to me as an ordained United Methodist minister and ecumenist. With all of my education and experience I really had nothing to do with this ancient and essential revelation as found in this verse. Maybe if we had only the first three Gospels and Paul's writings some understandings could have kept more simple. But I am not complaining!

Twelve words, none even containing two syllables, strike us as a brilliant literary and theological statement. But surely there has to be more than that to convey the claims we make! A dozen words lay before you and me, revelation that boggles the mind and thrills the soul. On top of that they are so simple and require a reading level that causes some of us who have spent our lives reading many difficult words to shudder in amazement. It must mean our dear Lord wants everyone to have access to His Word and that is not to imply ordained clergy are unneeded.

So, *we are in touch with ancient and essential revelation*. How blessed we are to have the faithfullness of our spiritual Fathers!

CONCLUSION

The Lord's own flesh and blood (*food and drink*) are shared with us. We are not left totally in the dark as to the sublime and yet fundamental act of institution that has been left with us. The word "real" carries with it a powerful mystery and for most of us we are just beginning to get a handle on this far-reaching event enacted in our churches. Is Christ among us? Of course, and we are so privileged that we even get to share in his flesh and blood. Simple and consecrated elements are given the stamp of that originally revealed. You and I are participants in a drama of salvation that defies measurement. His own *food and drink*!

EXPLORATION

1. Why do you suppose Jesus used such simple — even imaginative — elements?

2. Have you ever wondered what your body and blood has to do with His?

3. Given the context of our simple verse, what does "real" mean to you?

4. How do you describe the closeness so piercingly communicated by "My" flesh and blood?

5. Who or what is responsible for upholding and implementing the revelation before us?

IV

REAL PRESENCE

*"Whoever eats my flesh and drinks my blood re-
mains in me, and I in Him."*   John 6:56 (NIV)

INTRODUCTION

There is a coming together and merging with the Lord that is
awesomely mysterious and profound.

To receive the Sacrament indicates we remain in Him and He
in us. So, we are brought to terms with something (Someone) in
more than a symbolic and figurative sense. Perhaps the best desig-
nation is *real presence*. This not only avoids such heavy terminol-
ogy as transubstantiation and consubstantiation but gives a work-
ing, simplified way of understanding a very difficult idea. Our
spiritual forebears, John and Charles Wesley, found this delinea-
tion appropriate. They were on solid ground because I believe it
would also fit what is intended to happen since the time of Christ
and the Apostles. *Real Presence* has a way of dispelling ideas that
maintain only symbolism and/or figurative language are present.
As is often the case in our pilgrimage, we strain for words to tell us
some aspect of truth and discover some are better than others but
all are somewhat lacking! Yet, we do have beacons under the guidance of the Holy Spirit over the centuries and we are blessed!

FOCUS

The special occasion or worship activity we label Holy Communion somehow and some way calls into being an incomparable
oneness in Christ. It is as though to swallow the bread and wine is
to allow Him to enter our bodies with His blood flowing through

our arteries and veins, yes, and vice versa! Allowing for the inadequacy of language, let us name what we mean.

APPLICATION

There is power transcending our understanding

Don't you feel like saying, "Are we dealing with nuclear energy or some primeval resource?" Maybe your true thoughts are along these lines: "This is just too irrational and I would rather hear about something else" or "Why deal with something so nebulous and probably unimportant?" It is said by some we should stay away from politics and religion because they always start arguments. We might even pursue this further but of what value would that be in light of the fact our Lord says, also in John's Gospel: "If you hold to my teaching, you are really my disciples. Then you will know the truth, and the truth will set you free." We are intended to struggle and yet rest assured in a peace that passes all understanding. There is a banquet on the altar of the Lord that promises eucharistic might. O sing of the greatness found in these words written by a contemporary Liberian: "Come, let us eat, for now the feast is spread" and "Come, let us drink, for now the wine is poured."

If you are like I am, I want things much more neatly put into an understandable package than this verse. After all, we know — for the most part — what is meant by our Master telling us to "love your enemies and pray for those who persecute you"! Yes, and the whole idea of power is much more easy to digest, provided we can circumvent special terms like *real presence* applied to the Lord's Supper. I believe much of the time as clergy and laity, we prefer power on the basis of something we can perceive as a worldly benefit. What will it take to push membership and worship, plus salary level, to a place where brothers and sisters say, "He or she is such a success"?

So, *there is a power transcending our understanding.* I beg of you not to turn away in frustration.

There is a love that wants us to be Christlike.

Jesus doesn't just want to hug us tightly; He wants to become part of us and vice versa. His goal is that of His love penetrating us and encompassing us. In a sense we are Him and He is us. See how priceless the Holy Communion is! The world had never and has never known such love. We find the gift of His very life in the Sacrament. We are privileged to have His *real presence*. In a way this love is "in, among, for, with us." The heavens shout: "Love divine, all loves excelling" and "Fix in us thy humble dwelling." "Love" is such a misused term today, so we need with urgency to embrace fully what our wondrous Savior and Lord has in store for those who confess Him.

It needs continual repeating that "the" Sacrament is a means of spiritual formation par excellence. Why? Primarily because God is love and His Son comes to us in His Body and Blood. How can we be formed into His image without special — even miraculous — worship times that hold high the Lord's Supper? The truth of the matter is we probably cannot be; that does not put down those claiming Christ who find "sacrament" secondary to the preaching event and/or disciplined prayer. The point is: Why digress from our Lord's command to remember Him in a certain way, especially when so deeply-imbedded in Holy Scriptures?

So, *there is a love that wants us to be Christlike.* We are called to be like Him in thought, word, and deed.

There is a joy beyond worldly appreciation.

Perhaps we have all heard Christians are "in" the world but not "of" the world. It remains a helpful way of seeing ourselves as a peculiar people God has called. Saint Paul helps us when he says in Romans twelve: "Do not conform any longer to the pattern of this world ... " Christians are a select — even an elite — group in the best sense of the word. Certainly a precious highlight and even defining moment is found in the Holy Communion. When we receive His Body and Blood, we sometimes weep in a joy that is so foreign to anything the world can appreciate. As we receive the elements, we can know in our innermost beings our sins are forgiven and heaven our eventual home! Why? He is in us and we are in Him.

In times of turbulence and travail our oldest daughter used to speak of her great desire for joy. It was that noteworthy moment(s) that the Father not only smiled from heaven on His children but especially upon her. As you and I are being blessed by the Eucharist, there is that Fatherly smile from heaven that is known only by His sons and daughters in the Body of Christ. When Saint Paul lists the fruit of the Spirit in Galatians five, joy is second only to love. We are joyful about Christ's death and the death of our sins. Why? Because His Crucifixion means salvation, redemption, and resurrection. Our sins are no more, unless we choose to re-embrace them. Sadness becomes joy. Indeed, death becomes life.

So, *there is a joy beyond worldly appreciation.* Celebrate your select place before the Father, the Son, and the Holy Spirit.

There is a grace overcoming but utilizing our weakness.

Times of sharing coffee and cookies with conversation are often helpfully soothing. Times of sharing soft drinks and pizza are just outright fun. Perhaps some even find beer and pretzels just "the ticket" to make life look better. If the Holy Spirit is present and who would doubt that possibility, we may very well be having a "grace filled" occasion. But, as Christians, if this is all we have in our lives, we have a colossal problem. Holy Communion provides a unique grace that in a way overwhelms and conquers. It is also grace that makes "the " Sacrament possible, In our frailty we need much more than the above mentioned pleasant times, as important as they may appear. Our deepest need calls for somebody or Someone far bigger and better to do for us what we can never do for ourselves.

Grace enables me to remain in Him and He in me. What pitiful creatures we are without this favor of the Father through the Son! Jesus the Christ gives His all that we might have life and have it abundantly. The universal appeal of the hymn, "Amazing Grace," is that it seems to speak directly to all of us. Indeed, "How sweet the sound that saved a wretch like me!" Then, the first stanza goes on to say, "I once was lost, but now am found; was blind, but now I see." Our weakness is God's great opportunity. His Body and His Blood provide His *real presence*. Oh, sing to your Lord a new song of being a "very important person" in His sight, sealed by His unmerited favor.

So, *there is a grace overcoming but utilizing our weakness.* Christians call it His *real presence*.

There is a faithfulness allowing no defeat.

Real presence strongly indicates that our Lord is faithfully present in a way that no one else is. "The" Sacrament is the center-piece of understanding and appreciating the fact there is no ulti-mate defeat for those who cling tenaciously to His Body and His Blood. This is a glorious experience that is shared by those spiri-tual ancestors coming out of the First Century and continuing with-out interruption even to the moment we share now. In my own weak and ineffectual way I attempt to visualize my brothers/sisters across the ages receiving the Lord's Supper. They are from all races and nationalities. They come from every social and eco-nomic class. Their political sensitivities embrace every shade in a rainbow. They are saints and sinners. They are saintly sinners and sinful saints! Truly we are one in the Spirit and one in the Lord at His table.

Unless there is faithfulness over the long haul, there just isn't much else. Power, love, joy, and grace speak of *real presence*. Yet, what if there is a lack of faithfulness? So much tends to de-pend on so few! We speak of discipline and commitment. We speak of consistency and persistency. We speak of an attitude that maintains, "When the going gets tough, the tough get going." The eternal Son of the eternal Father became a man, born of the Blessed Virgin Mary, and lived among us. Since that time He lives among us through His Body and Blood. He does so through the faithful ministrations of "the" Sacrament by the ordained clergy under the guidance of the Holy Spirit.

So, *there is a faithfulness allowing no defeat.* Persecute or kill us but we shall never be overpowered by the Evil One.

CONCLUSION

The term *real presence* seems more and more to be coming into usage today among those serious about religion, especially the Holy Communion. I believe this is very healthy and spiritually wholesome. It is a term that certainly isn't new and yet it has such a contemporary ring to it. Furthermore, it communicates in ways beneficially across denominational lives. The promise of whoever eats His flesh and drinks His blood being pivotal in His residence in us, plus our remaining in Him, causes us to be thankful many times over. I like all of this just that way, don't you?

EXPLORATION

1. How do you understand the power in "the" Sacrament?

2. Have you ever experienced the love Christ intends in His Supper?

3. At what times in your life is joy most noticeable?

4. Why do you suppose we are all dependent on His grace?

5. When was the last time you were convinced it was "okay" to give up?

V

LIVING FATHER

*"Just as the living Father sent me and I live be-
cause of the Father, so the one who feeds on me
will live because of me."*   John 6:57 (NIV)

INTRODUCTION

The *living Father* comes to the forefront and we get the distinct impression the living Son receives His life from the Father.

We are now exposed to the inner and intimate workings of the Holy Trinity. God chooses to come to us or relate to us as Father, Son, and Holy Spirit. Three eternal beings work together as one and yet are separate and explicit. Jesus clearly states He is dependent on the Father and the Father is not dependent on Him, except as the Father chooses to be. In a mysterious fashion the Holy Spirit embraces both for as Jesus says in John Fourteen: "And I will ask the Father, and he will give you another Counselor to be with you forever — the Spirit of Truth." These are not easy words for us to understand in today's seemingly overpowering attitude — even among Christians — that whatever works for you theologically is fine. It is as we seriously in prayer and abandonment enter into the very life of the Holy Trinity we recognize the super-human life of One in three, who are also three in One. I know of no single act of worship that delineates this for us more carefully than the Holy Communion. At the Eucharist all three are present!

FOCUS

We embark on a journey at once really beyond our comprehensions and yet very simply put before us. We discover a Father/

Son relationship so awesome we may even wonder about the terms. However, our choice is quite clear. Perhaps the best way to get a hold of this truth is to utilize a bit of creative alliteration.

APPLICATION

The Father does a marvelous thing for
his sons and daughters.

Think of the splendor of Holy Communion! I really am not thinking of massive and historic cathedrals or intricate liturgical services. I am envisioning a precious service instituted by our Lord, wherever it is celebrated. Very expensive chalices may be breath-taking but isn't the point that the holy Blood of Christ be transmit-ted to the worshiper, regardless of the container? Is there any more power and love with elements on an ornate altar costing in the thousands than a plain wooden one made by a poor farmer in Peru? The world tends to identify outward and costly channels of wor-ship as somehow more pleasing to God. Not so! The Father through His Son gives His sons and daughters a marvelous gift. In one of the Great Thanksgivings the celebrant says, "Father, you loved the world so much that in the fullness of time you sent your only Son to be our Savior."

While we receive the Body and Blood of Christ, we are reminded by our Savior that it all begins with His Father, your Father, my Father, and indeed our Father. The universal Nicene Creed professes: "We believe in one God, the Father, the Almighty, maker of heaven and earth, of all that is seen and unseen." The Eucharist is the center of our marvelous relationship with God the Father, Son, and Holy Spirit. "The" Father always comes before the other two. In the opening lines of the Liturgy of the Catechimens from the Divine Liturgy of Saint John the Chrysostom the priest says: "Blessed be the Kingdom of the Father, and of the Son, and of the Holy Spirit, now and ever, and to the ages of ages." Jesus is first of all sent by the *living Father* and He lives in us because of the Father.

So, *the Father does a marvelous thing for His sons and daughters*. On orders from Him, Jesus brings into being the Holy Communion.

The Son provides a majestic glimpse into the meaning of His Supper.

It is as though Jesus is inviting us by saying, "Please come to My Supper but remember I live because of the *Living Father* and He is the One who really makes it possible." There is such majesty in all of this! Jesus is King of all kings because of the *living father*. I dare say this is a glimpse into "the" Sacrament at once some mystifying and yet clarifying. This does not dilute or destroy the deity of Jesus Christ; it does take Holy Scripture at face value and allow it to speak fully. We feed and live on Christ but it is done with the Father's full approval. It is also done, recognizing and giving thanks for the Source that is not dependent on any source. Our Lord takes us into lofty regions where mysticism and mystery reside that point to creation itself. We may feel at this moment we have a desire to come up for air. We begin to probe the life of the Father and the Son, plus the relationship between the two.

Sometimes I feel Jesus is maintaining, "Hang on, now, I want to tell you something absolutely necessary to get a more full and complete understanding of 'the' Sacrament." If we are really attuned to what is happening, I believe our hearts are all aflutter as we are privileged to enter where the "holy of holies" dwells. It requires being on His wavelength and spiritually being taken into a land punctuated by sighs too deep for words to communicate. The Father desires that precious human beings know His Son in an intimate way and on a regular basis. Let us no longer complain about our spiritual plight! We have His Body and Blood.

So, *the Son provides a majestic glimpse into the meaning of His Supper*. Fatherly goodness surrounds and pervades the entire event.

The Holy Spirit calls into being this
magnificent, ongoing celebration.

We sense and are prodded to come to worship in order to receive the Lord's Supper. "Do not resist the Holy Spirit" is conveyed to us in many ways in Holy Scripture. Perhaps the classic expression is found in Saint Paul's Letter to the Church at Ephesus in the fourth chapter: "And do not grieve the Holy Spirit of God, with whom you were sealed for the day of redemption." We are called to the magnificence of a happening so wondrous we receive the Savior of the ages! While His sacrifice is once and for all time, the Holy Spirit enables it to happen over and over again that we may receive nourishment for our very souls.

In the "Great Thanksgiving for General Use" that appears in the publication *At The Lord's Table: A Communion Service Book of Use by the Minister* (Abingdon) I am enthralled by a magnificence beyond me as I say: "Send the power of your Holy Spirit on us and these gifts, that in the breaking on this bread and the drinking of this wine we may know the presence of the living Christ ... " It seems as though my whole duty in ministry hits its mark there and then. In the publication *Come, Holy Spirit* (Evangel Press) the same sacred sense engulfs me as I proclaim: "Holy Father, send the power of Your Holy Spirit on us and these gifts of bread and wine that they may become the body and blood of our Savior and Lord." The *epiclesis* or invoking of the Holy Spirit is so sublime I seem to be blissfully caught between heaven and earth!

So, *the Holy Spirit calls into being this magnificent, ongoing celebration*. Again, we pause to say humbly, "Thank You," as best we can.

The Holy Trinity gives us a magnanimous banquet.

Indeed, we are given a very generous — even beyond our comprehension — table of food and drink! The Father, Son, and Holy Spirit are perfectly united. The angels sing and the saints who have gone before us are out in joy! We feed on the Son of the *living Father.* We live because Jesus the Christ gives to us His Body and Blood. Talk about generosity! It is a feast that goes far beyond the finest food and drink any chef could prepare! No restaurant even on the jet set circuit could come with such a sumptuous and elegant meal. Come worshipers, the Holy Trinity has lovingly co-operated in complete perfection to bring you that which the world cannot and can never give. The very Savior of His people is among them and He gives them the most precious gift of all: Himself.

As you can see, to wax eloquently in gratitude and humility with sincerity still leaves an infinite number of words unspoken. I love Eucharistic Prayer 111 as found in the Roman Catholic order of Mass:

> Father, you are holy indeed,
> and all creation rightly gives you praise.
> All life, all holiness comes from you
> through your Son, Jesus Christ our Lord,
> by the working of the Holy Spirit.
> From age to age you gather a people to
> yourself, so that from east to west a perfect
> offering may be made to the glory of your
> name.

When the God of all ages gives so generously a spiritual banquet, why should we ever be malnourished!

So, *the Holy Trinity gives to us a magnanimous banquet.* Perhaps we will yet learn faith answers for our lives are readily available.

The Father, Son, and Holy Spirit treat us to a masterful work of spiritual art.

Sometimes I discern the Lord saying to all clergy: "Do whatever is proper and in good taste in your worship services. But always remember to preach the Word and celebrate the Sacrament." What do you know and what can you even imagine more significant than that? If the most brilliant artist or a combination of many come together to a worship committee meeting, what could possibly be improved? The Eucharist has a way of lifting us out and away from self, plus minimizing the personality of the pastor or priest. Preaching alone in worship tends to place too much emphasis on an individual and his/her capabilities. Greatly inspired preaching can certainly be sacramental but is not "the" Sacrament.

Every movement of the Communion liturgy is intended to have the very breath of the Holy Spirit in it. It is an artist's dream of ongoing and unlimited creativity, It comes to us in rightly measured streams of mercy and perfectly portioned our rivulets of peace. The *living Father*, sometimes like a still small voice and sometimes like a thunder clap, says, "Let is happen," and it does. I doubt there is any more privileged person in this entire universe than the ordained pastor and/or priest celebrating this masterful work that is spiritual art at its best. Can you imagine? The Father, Son, and Holy Spirit are not only looking over your shoulder but in the deepest recesses of your soul!

So, *the Father, Son, and Holy Spirit treat us to a masterful work of spiritual art.* "God of grace and God of glory" ... "Grant us wisdom, grant us courage, for the facing of this hour."

CONCLUSION

As we read and study the New Testament, especially the Gospels, our Lord has a way of putting everything and everyone in perspective. Try to keep an attachment to five adjectives that aid us in our difficult topic: *marvelous, majestic, magnificent, magnanimous, and masterful.* I believe such descriptive words, while obviously inadequate, do give us important assistance. Most have probably heard "the more things change, the more they are the same." This is true with the *living Father*! We need to understand that the only perfect God/Man needed to pray to Someone. He did. His Father. "Our Father in heaven, hallowed be your name" and "My Father, if it is possible, may this cup be taken from me" reverberate through our precious Faith.

EXPLORATION

1. How would you go about describing the Father?

2. What does it mean that we feed on Jesus?

3. Can you imagine "the" Sacrament without the Holy Spirit?

4. Have you ever seriously pondered what we call "The Holy Trinity"

5. Do you sense three eternal persons in Holy Communion?

VI

FROM HEAVEN

"This is the bread that came down from heaven.
Our forefathers ate manna and died, but he who
feeds on this bread will live forever."

John 6:58 (NIV)

INTRODUCTION

Our Blessed Savior and Lord wants us to know the holy sacrifice of Himself is of everlasting significance for humanity.

The closing words of this unusually awesome series of verses is placed before us. It is to show us that disciples of Jesus the Christ have available something (Someone) to them — wonder beyond wonders — that decidedly surpasses the manna of their forefathers. In the form of simple elements of the flesh of God, specifically the Son, is given to us to eat. He is *from heaven* and it is *from heaven*. It is another way of our Lord illustrating that He came "not to do away with the Law but to fulfill it." "Manna" was revelation in that day and time to the ancient Hebrews. It was not at all fully adequate and complete. Only His flesh (and blood) give us completeness and revelation which is definitive. Early disciples, especially Saint Paul, enabled the entire non-Jewish world also to have access to Him and consequently to the Holy Communion. "The" Sacrament is "a taste of glory" that comes *from heaven* and gives us a spiritual being and holiness of life our Lord's ancestors only dreamed about. Perhaps we want to maintain "But this is only idealism"; I believe we must not do that!

FOCUS

Our Savior and Lord places a capstone on His word to us about "the" Sacrament. We are not to look for something else as symbol and reality so powerfilled with love for those who seek to be like Him, indeed forever and ever. It seems to me our very best response is to state carefully affirmations that bring truth, life, and promise.

APPLICATION

We celebrate the greatness of the Father's everlasting gift found in the Lord's Supper.

"Celebration" is a key word in our vocabularies because it expresses from Christians a "shouting forth" of what has been done in the Incarnation. God came to us in flesh and blood. In the person of the Man of Galilee He was born among us; lived among us; ministered among us; died among us; arose among us; and ascended among us. His sacrifice on the Cross was truly among human beings who were seemingly hopelessly divided among themselves as to who He was and why He had come to be treated so brutally. In what sense could there be anything remotely resembling a celebration except for those who saw it as a victory in a power struggle? Little by little it became obvious you could kill a man like that but you really couldn't destroy Him. It also became more and more evident at the time of the Resurrection that His teaching would live beyond anyone's life who had witnessed such events. His sacrificial death would become a celebration!

The bread that came down *from heaven* would not only serve to exonerate Him in the eyes of some but provide a celebrative atmosphere for the ancient Body of Christ or the Church. For still others disappointment and even despair would set in because the crucified One was not dead at all. In the secrecy of homes and other places He would even come much alive through the celebration of His Supper! Heaven would touch earth and earth would touch heaven. It is known that some disciples simply seemed to live from one of His Suppers to the next. There was an urgency and a frequency that pervaded them. How can I go on living without my Savior and Lord? When can I partake of His precious Body and Blood again? They were unfamiliar with our theories and eroded basic meanings of "the" Sacrament. At face value they celebrated the Father's everlasting gift!

So, *we celebrate the greatness of the Father's everlasting gift found in the Lord's Supper*. With the Holy Spirit's prodding we need to celebrate more often!

We maintain the love of Jesus comes most perfectly in "the" Sacrament.

My guess is there are many professing His name who would argue with this affirmation. In fact, I know there are! Nevertheless, let us help them to jog their memories. Can the Resurrection have any serious validity apart from the Crucifixion? Dare we ever separate these two events in our appreciation of the Faith? Isn't laying down your life for your friends (and enemies) the apex of the manifestation of love? Jesus gave totally and completely of Himself in a humbling event before people who mocked and scorned Him. What else could He have given? He evaded and avoided worldly adulation to hang upon the Cross, even refusing to call upon legions of His Father's helpers to save Him. What else could he have done? He was perfectly obedient — even unto the Cross — because that was the will of the Father. What else could be expected of the Son who came from the heavens to live an earthly life not at all befitting of One sharing in the Holy Trinity. The love found in His Body and Blood calls us forever to a love that refuses to be limited in how far it will go for us.

This perfect love finds its expression in a simple and yet sublime act of worship. It came *from heaven*. It is profoundly personal in the sense each professing person partakes with his/her own agenda and presuppositions. It is powerfully communal as groups — regardless of numbers — receive His holy Body and Blood that binds them together in the loving energy of the Holy Spirit. How can we possibly know Him and have deep appreciation for His Resurrection unless we die with Him? For you and me this bread *from heaven* that lives forever is "the" Sacrament that has no equals.

We must not eat the old manna and die in our sins. It comes in many forms — even in our churches — and is inevitably beguiling!

So, *we maintain the love of Jesus comes most perfectly in "the" Sacrament.* I plead with you not to deny or belittle it!

We believe there is reality — not mere idealism — in His Body and Blood.

I suspect most of us have heard, "Christianity is a fine thing but just won't work" or variations. Likewise we have heard the retort in one form or another: "But have you tried it!" The problem of dealing with the "ideal" or "what should be" and the "real" or "what is" is ever with us. Our task is to be honest but never underestimate or blur the revelation to us. You and I can promise many things based on Holy Scripture. What we cannot do is to tell God what He can or cannot do! This is an ongoing spiritual phenomenon and means our faith in the Lord Jesus simply has to see us through. Can the "ideal" become the "real" in given situations? I believe it can. I also believe this is particularly true of the Lord's Supper. Some of our quandary is reduced to two questions: Are we prepared to take Holy Communion by coming to His table expectantly and openly? Are we aware that we are as privileged as the early disciples and saints? If we can give an unconditional affirmation to both, I firmly believe His Body and Blood become for us bread *from heaven.*

In our day and time it has become too easy to push the ideal understanding as witnessed to by the Ancient Church into a corner of irrelevancy. Our Lord did not institute "the" Sacrament for a given period of time or tell us we would eventually outgrow it! Yes, there is reality here and now for those who need His Body and Blood. Here is a "leap of faith" for all of us, at the same time the "one, holy, catholic apostolic" Church and the Gospels — plus Saint Paul's writing — convey to us what must never be pigeon holed in the miscellaneous section of our religious consciousness.

Don't deny the efficacy of "the" Sacrament by shrugging it off as so much idealism.

So, *we believe there is reality — not mere idealism — in the Body and Blood.* What comes *from heaven* is practically intended for our spiritual nurture and power!

We confess our ongoing need to grow in the understanding we receive bread from heaven.

I know of no single act of worship that radiates more blessed mystery than His Supper. Of course, this is why traditional Catholicism practices prayer before "the" Sacrament reserved in a tabernacle; there is the adoration of Christ's presence in the elements. However, I suggest to you, this is no reason for liberal Catholics and Protestants of many names to write off the need to be ever learning about such an exquisitely thrilling gift. I confess to you it takes lengthy meditation and even discouragement to break through a prevalent attitude of routine and complacency. How many television, radio and print media images imprint your brain every day? Probably this runs into the hundreds and thousands. How many images of a chalice and bread or cups and wafers or the Crucified One on the Cross imprint your brain on any given day? A culture that once aided and assisted Judeo-Christian values — for the most part — no longer does. In fact, quite the reverse is true and has been so now perhaps for two generations.

Read and re-read the key passages in the Gospels especially John 6:53-58, as well as Saint Paul's passages in First Corinthians. Read various translations and revisions. Memorize them and take them into your heart with gratitude. Prior to every service of Holy Communion call upon the Holy Spirit for guidance. Remember always to do so humbly and sincerely. One of the most helpful prayers of all is: "O Holy Spirit of God, take me as your disciple. Guide me, Illuminate me, sanctify me." Use Saturday night or early Sunday morning or both as a preparation time. Books like *The Imitation of Christ* by Thomas à Kempis are very helpful. In the section entitled "About the Blessed Sacrament" we read: "O

Jesus, sweetest, kindest, what great worship and thanksgiving we ought to show you, what never-ending praise, in return for your holy body! There is not a man to be found able to unfold in words its wonderful power."

So, *we confess our ongoing need to grow in the understanding we receive bread from heaven.* We plead with you, dear God, to teach us more!

We embrace with all our might the Eucharist that gives us Christ Himself.

We are called "to become" people of the Eucharist and then called "to be" people of the Eucharist! Let us eat His flesh and drink His blood! Let us become full of Him! Indeed, they are strange words for a society bloated with immoral and sacrilegious accesses. In a way they are even more strange for many professing His holy name who count "the" Sacrament of such little worth they would reduce to a bit of bread and a touch of grape juice the splendor of a heavenly banquet. May the Father forgive His children for treating the Eucharist slightly above an afternoon coffee break of pastry and coffee. Where is our greatness? It is found in the Christ. Where do we discover the Christ fully and completely giving Himself for us? In the Eucharist.

We are not starving sons and daughters with no bread *from heaven.* We are not Children languishing in thirst because the chalice is empty. We must embrace with all our might His Body and Blood are for those who truly believe that He is the Son of the Father who came to die for their sins. Can we not once again in droves around the world come repentently before His altar and receive "the" Sacrament? Can we not once again in droves leave His altar with tears of joy streaming down our cheeks? Can we not only do this weekly but daily in a world that daily seeks to take our Faith from us? We must hold Him tightly in love, gratitude, and obedience. That is possible! The Apostles, saints, martyrs, and disciples of the ages witness to that truth.

So, *we embrace with all our might the Eucharist that gives to us Christ Himself.* May our arms never grow tired of holding Him near and dear!

CONCLUSION

As we seek to pull into unity our visit together, we also are inspired to provide summary and substance to the words found in 6:53-58 of John's Gospel. They all seem to fit together in a perfect symphony, don't they? Whatever we have said in preceding sermons, in time they all communicate to us we Christians have bread *from heaven.* It is always more than we can scrutinize, analyze, or even finalize. Our affirmations can continue, spoken or unspoken. They will guide and direct us. They will help us always groping in a kind of heavenly painful joy, thrilling us forever to move onward and upward by the grace of almighty God! The Father calls through the eucharistic Body and Blood of His Son. The Holy Spirit in celestial sweetness and firm whispers says in love: "This *is* My Body; this *is* My Blood." Amen.

EXPLORATION

1. Do you know Holy Communion is a celebration?

2. Have you ever tried to measure Christ's love?

3. Why do we refuse the powerful reality of His Supper?

4. How can we keep growing as people of "the" Sacrament?

5. What hope do we have without our Lord, especially without His Body and His Blood?

Postlude

Pilgrim: You are so good to me! I yearn for "deeper things" and struggle away to achieve more knowledge. Then, you speak to me about grace and tell me that's all I need because Your power is made perfect in weakness. Lord, You are truly a miracle worker! Now, You have opened many doors for me. Now, I am beginning to learn something profound from the ages about John 6:53-58. I am so very grateful! Have I really come a long way or is my prideful self deceiving me again?

Jesus: In your own limited way you have put in print a beginning understanding of the Holy Sacrament. Being deceived by pride is very important. Place that in your memory.

Pilgrim: There is a certain ecstasy to Your agony during those final days, Lord. No creative genius can really depict them. The unique power of Your Body and Blood given for us causes me to shout for joy. But it also causes me to tremble. Just to be lost in such power and boundless love is at times all I desire. Forgive me, Lord, but there is a sadness that enters my heart and mind. It makes me so sad many in our churches just don't seem to understand — even to small degree — this gift that is allowed to be trapped in various kinds of wrappers. Please, I plead, enlighten me.

Jesus: My son, human sin and its depths are always with us. Do not lose heart. I call upon you to share with others the tiny truth I have enabled you to see. Remember to give away what you have been given.

Pilgrim: My Lord and my God, why is it You always have just the right words? I already know the answer. It is because You are fully God and fully man. It is because no one in all history is Your equal. It is because in You and only You we find our salvation. How privileged we are to have Saint John's message, breathed by the Holy Spirit of the living God! Just a few verses bring to us more joy, strength, and goodness than all the trillions of words spoken by countless famous people. I am humbled by having access to the Sacrament. I am even more humbled by being in a position to celebrate "for and among" Your needy children. Please help me to be worthy.

Jesus: Your thoughts come from the soul of one on the verge of serious spiritual growth in My will and ways. I will continue to guide you but stay close. The Devil is not pleased with your progress.

Pilgrim: Strange as it may seem, Lord, I feel at peace with myself. Yes, the Devil will visit me again. I pray the Holy Spirit will sustain me and I can be victorious. It will not happen in my own strength and I have to learn that again and again ... painfully! Please allow me to experience such interior peace more often. The tensions and frustrations of life deplete my energy all too often. Oh, Your Body and Your Blood, Lord, how stupendously wonderful they are! Such love and mercy are embodied in simple elements. Truly, when the Sacrament is celebrated and we receive it, all the demons in hell must cringe in horror. Words fail me, Lord. My thoughts and feelings have moved beyond saying what I experience.

Jesus: Be assured I know what you think and feel. Be assured of my everlasting love. I remind you: stay close. The Devil despises My Body and My Blood.

Pilgrim: Lord, I am spiritually exhausted for the first time in my life. Perhaps I have now lost my life and have now found it. Perhaps I know at last that to obey Your teaching is really to be Your disciple. Perhaps I know what it means to go in through the narrow gate. I repay You the only way I know how. I offer myself as a living sacrifice, trusting in Your Body and Your Blood.

Jesus: My Father and I are in perfect unity. Eternity belongs to us, along with the Holy Spirit. Be faithful.

Pilgrim: I believe that if I had only the verses from John 6:53-58 the rest of my life would be meaningful and fruitful. Of course, I know, dear Lord, there is much more to learn from these verses. Please make me a blessing to every life that I touch. Please continue to teach me. Please empower me at all times and all places to be Your person, speaking the truth in love. Please keep me in harmony with the Holy Spirit. It is true, Lord, that whether I live or die I belong to You and Your Supper provides ongoing spiritual strength. I pray You will satisfy my hunger and thirst, now and for evermore.

Jesus: Do not worry or fret, only cling tenaciously to Me.